LOVE

— IN —

MARRIAGE

Pope Francis on living and growing in love

Dear T,   1/6/20

I love being on this journey
with you. The page to the left
is what we started with as a
couple, and it continues to be
true today. Looking forward to
what the future may hold for us
together. You are my one +
true love. Love you always,

O'B

MAGNIFICAT®

CONTENTS

CONTENTS

PART TWO: GROWING IN CONJUGAL LOVE

FOREWORD

In April 2016, Pope Francis offered the world a magnificent wedding present: the Apostolic Exhortation* *The Joy of Love—Amoris laetitia*—issued following two bishops' synods* on the family.

A text of such scope is a veritable treasure for families and for the Church. But this treasure isn't easily accessible: its length (nearly 250 pages), the language (sometimes very specific), and the complexity of the questions it tackles can, for some readers, be an obstacle. And that's such a shame!

With a particular concern for pedagogy, the pope clearly states: "I do not recommend a rushed reading of the text. The greatest benefit, for families themselves and for those engaged in the family apostolate,* will come if each part is read patiently and carefully, or if attention is paid to the parts dealing with their specific needs. It is likely, for example, that married couples will be more concerned with Chapters Four and Five" (7).

This booklet, which presents chapter 4 of the exhortation, thus seeks to fulfill the pope's wish that as many as possible should discover or rediscover the beauty of love within marriage and its fruitfulness.

Chapter 4 is presented in two parts, following the same structure as the pope's text:

• Part one: Our everyday love

This first part covers paragraphs 90 to 119. It constitutes a remarkable, very detailed commentary on Saint Paul's Letter to the Corinthians, commonly known as the hymn of charity*

(1 Cor 13:4-7). This text, so often heard at the celebration of the sacrament* of marriage, here unfolds its significance, in all its depth, for the human couple: the qualities of true love.

• Part two: Growing in conjugal charity

The second part, corresponding to paragraphs 120 to 164, offers Pope Francis' reflections on the growth of everyday conjugal love throughout our lives.

For each section of the pope's text, you will find, first of all, a general question, to be looked at even before reading the text, then, at the end of the section, a series of questions about the text, followed by questions about your own life to help delve deeper into the text. Finally, an invitation to prayer concludes the period of reflection. Whether alone, as a couple, or as a group, the goal is to let oneself be questioned by the thinking of the pope and the Church, and to better assimilate it.

At the end of this booklet, you will find a glossary, notes about the authors quoted, and a list of the biblical books referred to in this chapter of the exhortation.

We hope this booklet will make a lovely gift for parishes, friends, or family to offer to engaged couples or newlyweds. It is certainly a beautiful aid for deepening the conjugal love of those who, already united by the sacrament of marriage, are struggling or going through difficult times, as well as those experiencing the large and the small joys of family life. It also allows each one of us to discover the good news offered by the Church about the grandeur of human love.

Father Arnaud Toury

* Words followed by an asterisk can be found in the glossary, pp. 123-124.

HOW TO USE THIS BOOKLET:

• A preliminary question

Before beginning this journey, it may be helpful for everyone to clearly state their expectations of this period of study and sharing based on the pope's text, and to make a note of them to regularly refer back to.

• As a couple

The themes dealt with in this text are very personal, even for a couple, and care should be taken to show great tact and respect during the various exchanges. Each one of us has our own personal history. Some subjects may perhaps be too painful for one spouse to want to open up about immediately. It is very important to respect this by avoiding interrupting each other or probing too deeply into difficult subjects.

• As a group

Studying this text in a group can be a source of great dialogue and support. However, certain points raised by the pope are the exclusive domain of a couple's private life, or even that of an individual spouse. This is why, in group reflection, time must be set aside for sharing as a couple, at the start and at the end of each reflection (so that requests for forgiveness, for example, may be made in total confidence). Another way of handling a group approach might be to get together once a month, leaving it up to each couple to reflect and talk in the meantime. This ensures that no one goes deeply into the text in complete isolation, while at the same time respecting each participant's own personal pace. It also allows couples to talk beforehand about what they wish to share in a group about the fruit of their reflections.

• Prayer

In all of these areas, prayer allows us to open ourselves up to the gifts of God for each of us. To begin each period of sharing, a simple prayer such as the following might be said:

Lord, you so love us that you gave us a heart capable of loving: guide our love to become ever more like yours. Pour your Holy Spirit into our hearts and onto our lips, that this time of sharing may open us to your grace and grant us to bear fruit that will remain.

> Strive eagerly for
> the greatest spiritual gifts.
> But I shall show you
> a still more excellent way.

(1 Cor 12:31)

OUR DAILY LOVE

89 All that has been said so far would be insufficient to express the Gospel of marriage and the family, were we not also to *speak of love*. For we cannot encourage a path of fidelity and mutual self-giving without encouraging the growth, strengthening, and deepening of conjugal and family love. Indeed, the grace of the sacrament of marriage is intended before all else "to perfect the couple's love."[1] Here too we can say that *even if I have faith so as to remove mountains, but have not love, I am nothing. If I give all I have, and if I deliver my body to be burned, but have not love, I gain nothing* (1 Cor 13:2-3). The word "love," however, is commonly used and often misused.[2]

OUR DAILY LOVE

IN A FEW SIMPLE WORDS, HOW WOULD I DEFINE LOVE?

90   In a lyrical passage of Saint Paul, we see some of the features of true love:

Love is patient,
love is kind;
love is not jealous or boastful;
it is not arrogant or rude.
Love does not insist on its own way,
it is not irritable or resentful;
it does not rejoice at wrong,
but rejoices in the right.
Love bears all things,
believes all things,
hopes all things,
endures all things
(1 Cor 13:4-7)

Love is experienced and nurtured in the daily life of couples and their children. It is helpful to think more deeply about the meaning of this Pauline text and its relevance for the concrete situation of every family.

REFLECT

ON THE TEXT

• Among the qualities of love given
by Saint Paul, which one seems to me
the most important?

• What moments in Christ's life
does each of them make me think of?

ABOUT MY LIFE

• Which are the qualities mentioned
that seem easiest for me personally
to put into practice?

• Which are the ones
I have difficulties with?

• Which are the ones that seem
most desirable to me?

TO CONCLUDE

• What request do I wish
to make of Christ?

SINCE THERE IS
more joy in giving than in receiving, teach us, Lord,
to rejoice in admiring each other's gifts, which in no way
detract from what we are, but, on the contrary,
mutually enrich us.

LOVE IS PATIENT

WHAT THOUGHTS DOES THE TITLE OF THIS SECTION
INSPIRE IN ME? AT FIRST GLANCE, IN WHAT WAY DOES
THIS SUBJECT SEEM IMPORTANT TO ME?

91 The first word used is *makrothyméi*. This does not simply have to do with *enduring all things*, because we find that idea expressed at the end of the seventh verse. Its meaning is clarified by the Greek translation of the Old Testament, where we read that God is *slow to anger* (Ex 34:6; Nm 14:18). It refers, then, to the quality of one who does not act on impulse and avoids giving offense. We find this quality in the God of the Covenant,* who calls us to imitate him also within the life of the family. Saint Paul's texts using this word need to be read in the light of the Book of Wisdom* (cf. 11:23; 12:2, 15-18), which extols God's restraint, as leaving open the possibility of repentance, yet insists on his power, as revealed in his acts of mercy.* God's *patience*, shown in his mercy towards sinners, is a sign of his real power.

92 Being patient does not mean letting ourselves be constantly mistreated, tolerating physical aggression, or allowing other people to use us. We encounter problems whenever we think that relationships or people ought to be perfect, or when we put ourselves at the center and expect things to turn out our way. Then everything makes us impatient, everything makes us react aggressively. Unless we cultivate patience, we will always find excuses for responding angrily. We will end up incapable of living together, antisocial, unable to control our impulses, and our families will become battlegrounds. That is why the word of God tells us: *Let all bitterness and wrath and anger and clamor and slander be put away from you, with all malice* (Eph 4:31). Patience takes root when I recognize that other people also have a right to live in this world, just as they are. It does not matter if they hold me back, if they unsettle my plans or annoy me by the way they act or think, or if they are not everything I want them to be. Love always has an aspect of deep compassion that leads to accepting the other person as part of this world, even when he or she acts differently than I would like. ▬

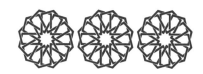

REFLECT

ON THE TEXT

• On what dimensions of patience does the pope insist?

• What surprises me?

• What in this text has touched you the most deeply?

ABOUT MY LIFE

• In what way does this section concern me?

• How do I live this dimension in my marriage,
and in my relationships with others?

• Do I welcome patience as a grace from God?

• When do patience and mercy seem to me
a sign of weakness?

• What are the reasons for my moments of impatience
and lack of indulgence toward others?

• How do I show compassion?

TO CONCLUDE

• What request do I have to present to God?

WITH MY SPOUSE OR IN THE QUIET OF MY HEART,
I want to say: I thank you... I'm sorry... Please...

—

LORD JESUS,
cleanse us of outbursts, anger, bitterness,
and malice in all its forms.

LOVE IS AT
THE SERVICE OF OTHERS

WHAT LINKS DO WE MAKE
BETWEEN LOVE AND SERVICE?

93 The next word that Paul uses is *chrestéuetai*. The word is used only here in the entire Bible. It is derived from *chrestós*: a good person, one who shows his goodness by his deeds. Here, in strict parallelism with the preceding verb, it serves as a complement. Paul wants to make it clear that patience is not a completely passive attitude, but one accompanied by activity, by a dynamic and creative interaction with others. The word indicates that love benefits and helps others. For this reason it is translated as *kind*; love is ever ready to be of assistance.

94 Throughout the text, it is clear that Paul wants to stress that love is more than a mere feeling. Rather, it should be understood along the lines of the Hebrew verb "to love"; it is "to do good." As Saint Ignatius of Loyola said, "Love is shown more by deeds than by words."[3] It thus shows its fruitfulness and allows us to experience the happiness of giving, the nobility and grandeur of spending ourselves unstintingly, without asking to be repaid, purely for the pleasure of giving and serving.

REFLECT

ON THE TEXT

• When I think about love, do I associate it
with the idea of service?

• How does the pope associate the idea
of service with love?

ABOUT MY LIFE

• Through what words and gestures do I express
goodness in my marriage and in my family?

• Do I serve with love? Does service seem to me
a condition for living at peace?

• Have I already experienced joy in serving?

• Am I aware that in serving I express my love?

TO CONCLUDE

• Which important point could become
a source for my prayer?

WITH MY SPOUSE OR IN THE QUIET OF MY HEART,
I want to say: I thank you... I'm sorry... Please...

—

LORD JESUS,
you said: *If I, therefore, the master and teacher,
have washed your feet, you ought to wash one another's
feet* (Jn 13:14). Help us to practice loving service
in our daily lives as you did.

LOVE IS NOT JEALOUS

HOW WOULD I DEFINE ENVY
IN THE RELATIONSHIP OF A COUPLE?

95 Saint Paul goes on to reject as contrary to love an attitude expressed by the verb *zelói*—to be jealous or envious. This means that love has no room for discomfiture at another person's good fortune (cf. Acts 7:9; 17:5). Envy is a form of sadness provoked by another's prosperity; it shows that we are not concerned for the happiness of others but only with our own well-being. Whereas love makes us rise above ourselves, envy closes us in on ourselves. True love values the other person's achievements. It does not see him or her as a threat. It frees us from the sour taste of envy. It recognizes that everyone has different gifts and a unique path in life. So it strives to discover its own road to happiness, while allowing others to find theirs.

96 In a word, love means fulfilling the last two commandments of God's Law*: *You shall not covet your neighbor's house; you shall not covet your neighbor's wife, or his manservant, or his maidservant, or his ox, or his donkey, or anything that is your neighbor's* (Ex 20:17). Love inspires a sincere esteem for every human being and the recognition of his or her own right to happiness. I love this person, and I see him or her with the eyes of God, who gives us everything *for our enjoyment* (1 Tm 6:17).

As a result, I feel a deep sense of happiness and peace. This same deeply rooted love also leads me to reject the injustice whereby some possess too much and others too little.

It moves me to find ways of helping society's outcasts to find a modicum of joy. That is not envy, but the desire for equality.

Put on, then, as God's chosen ones,
holy and beloved, heartfelt
compassion, kindness, humility,
gentleness, and patience,
bearing with one another
and forgiving one another,
if one has a grievance against another;
as the Lord has forgiven you,
so must you also do.

(Col 3:12-13)

REFLECT

ON THE TEXT

• Can I identify with the feelings Pope Francis
is writing about?

• Why does envy provoke sadness?

• What does Pope Francis suggest we do to counter envy?

ABOUT MY LIFE

• In what situations have I felt proud of my spouse's
or my family's achievements? At what moments have
I valued my spouse's success?

• In what circumstances have I felt jealousy
within our life as a couple?

• Have I ever experienced joy at seeing my spouse
surpass me in some area or other?

TO CONCLUDE

• What steps can I take to keep envy at bay?

WITH MY SPOUSE OR IN THE QUIET OF MY HEART,
I want to say: I thank you... I'm sorry... Please...

—

LORD GOD,
blessed are you for your word of consolation: *Fear not,
for I have redeemed you; I have called you by name:
you are mine. Upon the palms of my hands I have
written your name. Because you are precious in my eyes
and glorious, and because I love you.*

LOVE IS NOT BOASTFUL

WHAT DOES THE THEME OF THIS SECTION INSPIRE IN ME?

97 The following word, *perpereúetai*, denotes vainglory, the need to be haughty, pedantic, and somewhat pushy. Those who love not only refrain from speaking too much about themselves, but are focused on others; they do not need to be the center of attention. The word that comes next—*physioútai*—is similar, indicating that love is not arrogant. Literally, it means that we do not become "puffed up" before others. It also points to something more subtle: an obsession with showing off and a loss of a sense of reality. Such people think that, because they are more "spiritual" or "wise," they are more important than they really are. Paul uses this verb on other occasions, as when he says that *knowledge puffs up,* whereas *love builds up* (1 Cor 8:1). Some think that they are important because they are more knowledgeable than others; they want to lord it over them. Yet what really makes us important is a love that understands, shows concern, and embraces the weak. Elsewhere the word is used to criticize those who are "inflated" with their own importance (cf. 1 Cor 4:18) but in fact are filled more with empty words than the real "power" of the Spirit (cf. 1 Cor 4:19).

98 It is important for Christians to show their love by the way they treat family members who are less knowledgeable about the

Faith, weak or less sure in their convictions. At times the opposite occurs: the supposedly mature believers within the family become unbearably arrogant. Love, on the other hand, is marked by humility; if we are to understand, forgive, and serve others from the heart, our pride has to be healed and our humility must increase. Jesus told his disciples that in a world where power prevails, each tries to dominate the other, but *it shall not be so among you* (Mt 20:26). The inner logic of Christian love is not about importance and power; rather, *whoever would be first among you must be your slave* (Mt 20:27). In family life, the logic of domination and competition about who is the most intelligent or powerful destroys love. Saint Peter's admonition also applies to the family: *Clothe yourselves, all of you, with humility towards one another, for "God opposes the proud, but gives grace to the humble"* (1 Pt 5:5). ▬

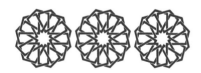

REFLECT

ON THE TEXT

- What words or expressions resonate with me?

- Why is boastfulness contrary to love?

- Where can a spirit of competition lead?

- What attitudes does the pope suggest
to avoid boastfulness?

ABOUT MY LIFE

- What part does humility play in my life?
Am I attentive to it?

- Can I name an instance when I have put aside my own
ideas in order to listen to and act on those of my spouse?

- How do I view my spouse? Other people?
Do I think myself "wiser," more "spiritual"; do I lecture
them or impose my knowledge?

- What does Jesus' attitude of humility inspire in me?

- Do I listen to others to understand their point of view
and learn from them?

TO CONCLUDE

- What element of this section prompts me to ask
for the strength of the Holy Spirit, the healing of an attitude,
of a fear, etc.?

WITH MY SPOUSE OR IN THE QUIET OF MY HEART,
I want to say: I thank you... I'm sorry... Please...

—

JOHN THE BAPTIST SAID:
He must increase; I must decrease. Lord Jesus, help us
on the path of self-renunciation, of welcoming the other,
and of openness to true love.

LOVE IS NOT RUDE

HOW DO WE MAKE A DISTINCTION BETWEEN LOVE AND GENTLENESS?

99 To love is also to be gentle and thoughtful, and this is conveyed by the next word, *aschemonéi*. It indicates that love is not rude or impolite; it is not harsh. Its actions, words, and gestures are pleasing and not abrasive or rigid. Love abhors making others suffer. Courtesy "is a school of sensitivity and disinterestedness" which requires a person "to develop his or her mind and feelings, learning how to listen, to speak and, at certain times, to keep quiet."[4] It is not something that a Christian may accept or reject. As an essential requirement of love, "every human being is bound to live agreeably with those around him."[5] Every day, "entering into the life of another, even when that person already has a part to play in our life, demands the sensitivity and restraint which can renew trust and respect. Indeed, the deeper love is, the more it calls for respect for the other's freedom and the ability to wait until the other opens the door to his or her heart."[6]

100 To be open to a genuine encounter with others, "a kind look" is essential. This is incompatible with a negative attitude that readily points out other people's shortcomings while overlooking one's own. A kind look helps us to see beyond our own limitations, to be patient and to cooperate with others, despite our differences. Loving kindness builds bonds, cultivates relationships, creates new networks of integration, and knits a firm social fabric. In this way, it grows ever stronger, for without a sense of belonging we cannot sustain a commitment to others; we end up seeking our convenience alone and life in common becomes impossible. Antisocial persons think that others exist only for the satisfaction of their own needs. Consequently, there is no room for the gentleness of love and its expression. Those who love are capable of speaking words of comfort, strength, consolation, and encouragement. These were the words that Jesus himself spoke: *Take heart, my son!* (Mt 9:2); *Great is your faith!* (Mt 15:28); *Arise!* (Mk 5:41); *Go in peace* (Lk 7:50); *Be not afraid* (Mt 14:27). These are not words that demean, sadden, anger, or show scorn. In our families, we must learn to imitate Jesus' own gentleness in our way of speaking to one another. ▬

Show yourself a model
of good deeds in every respect,
with integrity in your teaching,
dignity, and sound speech
that cannot be criticized.

(cf. Ti 2:7-8)

REFLECT

ON THE TEXT

• What words does the pope use to define gentleness?
Where does gentleness lead?

• What is a "kind look"?

ABOUT MY LIFE

• What loving words do I use to give comfort
and encouragement to those around me?

• Am I less gentle because I am afraid of being ridiculed
or of being used?

• Do I know how to recognize
the gentle attention of others to me?

• Do I consciously seek ways to be more pleasant,
courteous, respectful, and tactful
when I am with other people?

TO CONCLUDE

• After praying to the Holy Spirit, I ask Christ
for the strength to conquer a difficulty and I thank him
for having given me a natural talent.

WITH MY SPOUSE OR IN THE QUIET OF MY HEART,
I want to say: I thank you... I'm sorry... Please...

—

LORD,
grant that I seek not so much to be consoled as
to console, to be understood as to understand, to be loved
as to love. For, you have said, it is in giving that we receive
and in forgetting ourselves that we finds ourselves.

LOVE IS GENEROUS

HOW DO WE UNDERSTAND GENEROSITY?

101 We have repeatedly said that to love another we must first love ourselves. Paul's hymn to love, however, states that love *does not seek its own interest*, nor *seek what is its own*. This same idea is expressed in another text: *Let each of you look not only to his own interests, but also to the interests of others* (Phil 2:4). The Bible makes it clear that generously serving others is far more noble than loving ourselves. Loving ourselves is only important as a psychological prerequisite for being able to love others: *If a man is mean to himself, to whom will he be generous? No one is meaner than the man who is grudging to himself* (Sir 14:5-6).

102 Saint Thomas Aquinas explains that "it is more proper to charity to desire to love than to desire to be loved";[7] indeed, "mothers, who are those who love the most, seek to love more than to be loved."[8] Consequently, love can transcend and overflow the demands of justice, *expecting nothing in return* (Lk 6:35), and the greatest of loves can lead to *laying down one's life* for another (cf. Jn 15:13). Can such generosity, which enables us to give freely and fully, really be possible? Yes, because it is demanded by the Gospel: *You received without pay; give without pay* (Mt 10:8). ▬

"

This is my commandment:
love one another
as I love you.
No one has greater
love than this,
to lay down one's life
for one's friends. "

(Jn 15:12-13)

REFLECT

ON THE TEXT

• What kind of generosity is the pope speaking about?

• To love oneself, yet not to seek one's own interests:
How does the pope reconcile this apparent contradiction?

• What does it mean
"to give your life for the one you love"?

ABOUT MY LIFE

• How do I view myself? Positively, negatively?
Do I love myself as I am?

• Are there moments when an attachment to self,
or self-pity, keeps me from giving (my time,
a word of comfort, a favor, etc.)?

• What person, for me, is a model
of the gift of self to the end?

• Have I ever had the occasion to give something
without expecting anything in return?
What feelings did I have at the time?

• How do I react to the thought of giving
my life for my spouse?

TO CONCLUDE

• What seems necessary for me to clarify within myself?
What request do I wish to make of the Lord?

WITH MY SPOUSE OR IN THE QUIET OF MY HEART,
I want to say: I thank you... I'm sorry... Please...

—

LORD JESUS,
you proved to us that *no one has greater love than this,
to lay down one's life for one's friends*: grant us the grace
to imitate you.

LOVE IS NOT IRRITABLE OR RESENTFUL

THE POPE SPEAKS OF
"A VIOLENT REACTION WITHIN, A HIDDEN IRRITATION."
WHAT DOES THIS EXPRESSION SIGNIFY TO ME?

103 If the first word of Paul's hymn spoke of the need for a patience that does not immediately react harshly to the weaknesses and faults of others, the word he uses next—*paroxýnetai*—has to do more with an interior indignation provoked by something from without. It refers to a violent reaction within, a hidden irritation that sets us on edge where others are concerned, as if they were troublesome or threatening and thus to be avoided. To nurture such interior hostility helps no one. It only causes hurt and alienation. Indignation is only healthy when it makes us react to a grave injustice; when it permeates our attitude towards others it is harmful.

104 The Gospel tells us to look to the log in our own eye (cf. Mt 7:5). Christians cannot ignore the persistent admonition of God's word not to nurture anger: *Do not be overcome by evil* (Rom 12:21). *Let us not grow weary in doing good* (Gal 6:9). It is one thing to sense a sudden surge of hostility and another to give into it, letting it take root in our hearts: *Be angry but do not sin; do not let the sun go down on your anger* (Eph 4:26). My advice is never to let the day end without making peace in the family. "And how am I going to make peace? By getting down on my knees? No! Just by a small gesture, a little something, and harmony within your family will be restored. Just a little caress, no words are necessary. But do not let the day end without making peace in your family."⁹ Our first reaction when we are annoyed should be one of heartfelt blessing, asking God to bless, free, and heal that person. *On the contrary bless, for to this you have been called, that you may obtain a blessing* (1 Pet 3:9). If we must fight evil, so be it; but we must always say "no" to violence in the home. ▬

If I have the gift of prophecy and comprehend all mysteries and all knowledge; if I have all faith so as to move mountains but do not have love, I am nothing.

(1 Cor 13:2)

REFLECT

ON THE TEXT

• Why can indignation be just?

• When does resentment become harmful?

• What remedies for resentment
does the pope suggest?

ABOUT MY LIFE

• When anger seizes me when I am with my spouse
or someone else, what do I feel? How do I behave?

• In our life as a couple or as a family, how does the day end
after a quarrel? What do I do? What do I expect others to do?

• The pope invites us to say "no" to resentment by blessing.
Have I ever done that?

• Am I irritable? Do I let my outbursts of anger master me?

TO CONCLUDE

• What grabs my attention in this section
about which I might pray?

WITH MY SPOUSE OR IN THE QUIET OF MY HEART,
I want to say: I thank you... I'm sorry... Please...

—

LORD JESUS,
you ask that we not let the sun go down on our anger.
Grant us to find the words to extinguish anger and its
repercussions, and restore mutual confidence.
Teach us the art of blessing.

LOVE FORGIVES

WHAT ROLE DOES FORGIVENESS PLAY IN A COUPLE'S RELATIONSHIP?

105 Once we allow ill will to take root in our hearts, it leads to deep resentment. The phrase *ou logízetai to kakón* means that love "takes no account of evil"; "it is not resentful." The opposite of resentment is forgiveness, which is rooted in a positive attitude that seeks to understand other people's weaknesses and to excuse them. As Jesus said, *Father, forgive them; for they know not what they do* (Lk 23:34). Yet we keep looking for more and more faults, imagining greater evils, presuming all kinds of bad intentions, and so resentment grows and deepens. Thus, every mistake or lapse on the part of a spouse can harm the bond of love and the stability of the family. Something is wrong when we see every problem as equally serious; in this way, we risk being unduly harsh with the failings of others. The just desire to see our rights respected turns into a thirst for vengeance rather than a reasoned defense of our dignity.

106 When we have been offended or let down, forgiveness is possible and desirable, but no one can say that it is easy. The truth is that "family communion can only be preserved and perfected through a great spirit of sacrifice. It requires, in fact, a ready and generous openness of each and all to understanding, to forbearance, to pardon, to reconciliation. There is no family that does not know how selfishness, discord, tension, and conflict violently attack and at times mortally wound its own communion: hence there arise the many and varied forms of division in family life." [10]

107 Today we recognize that being able to forgive others implies the liberating experience of understanding and forgiving ourselves. Often our mistakes, or criticism we have received from loved ones, can lead to a loss of self-esteem. We become distant from others, avoiding affection, and fearful in our interpersonal relationships. Blaming others becomes falsely reassuring. We need to learn to pray over our past history, to accept ourselves, to learn how to live with our limitations, and even to forgive ourselves, in order to have this same attitude towards others.

108 All this assumes that we ourselves have had the experience of being forgiven by God, justified by his grace and not by our own merits. We have known a love that is prior to any of our own efforts, a love that constantly opens doors, promotes, and encourages. If we accept that God's love is unconditional, that the Father's love cannot be bought or sold, then we will become capable of showing boundless love and forgiving others even if they have wronged us. Otherwise, our family life will no longer be a place of understanding, support, and encouragement, but rather one of constant tension and mutual criticism. ▬

REFLECT

ON THE TEXT

• How does resentment set in? What feeds it?

• How does forgiveness stop the spread of bitterness?

• In what way does forgiveness allow
for communion between people?

• Why must we forgive ourselves? In what way
is the experience of God's forgiveness necessary?

• In what way does an emphasis on mistakes
damage the bond of love?

ABOUT MY LIFE

• Can I cite an occasion of forgiveness unconditionally
given, of forgiveness received? What benefits
did I draw from them?

• Do I know how to forgive myself
or do I let guilt overwhelm my conscience?

• Do I take the first step or
do I wait for the other person to come to me?

• Have I ever experienced God's mercy and tenderness?

• What is my attitude toward
my spouse's mistakes or faults?

TO CONCLUDE

• I take time to pray as I review my own personal history
in the sight of God and open myself to his forgiveness.

(This reflection may lead to a desire
for the Sacrament of Reconciliation.)

WITH MY SPOUSE OR IN THE QUIET OF MY HEART,
I want to say: I thank you... I'm sorry... Please...

—

LORD JESUS,
grant us to be simple, like King David, and say, *Yes,
I know my sin* (cf. Ps 51). Teach us to forgive the faults,
large and small, that wound us, just as we weed out
brambles from a path, one by one, to clear the way ahead.

Put on the new self,
created in God's way
in righteousness and holiness of truth.

Therefore, putting away falsehood,
speak the truth, each one to his neighbor,
for we are members of one another.
Be angry but do not let the sun set on your anger,
and do not leave room for the devil.

No foul language
should come out of your mouths,
but only such as is good for needed edification,
that it may impart grace to those who hear.

And do not grieve the holy Spirit of God,
with which you were sealed
for the day of redemption.

All bitterness, fury,
anger, shouting, and reviling
must be removed from you,
along with all malice.

[And] be kind to one another,
compassionate,
forgiving one another
as God has forgiven you in Christ.

(Eph 4:24-27, 29-32)

LOVE REJOICES
WITH OTHERS

WHERE THERE IS LOVE,
IT SEEMS NATURAL TO REJOICE WITH OTHERS.
WHAT COULD LIMIT THIS JOY?

109 The expression *chaírei epì te adikía* has to do with a negativity lurking deep within a person's heart. It is the toxic attitude of those who rejoice at seeing an injustice done to others. The following phrase expresses its opposite: *sygchaírei te aletheía*: "it rejoices in the right." In other words, we rejoice at the good of others when we see their dignity and value their abilities and good works. This is impossible for those who must always be comparing and competing, even with their spouse, so that they secretly rejoice in their failures.

110 When a loving person can do good for others, or sees that others are happy, they themselves live happily and in this way give glory to God, for *God loves a cheerful giver* (2 Cor 9:7). Our Lord especially appreciates those who find joy in the happiness of others. If we fail to learn how to rejoice in the well-being of others, and focus primarily on our own needs, we condemn ourselves to a joyless existence, for, as Jesus said, *it is more blessed to give than to receive* (Acts 20:35). The family must always be a place where, when something good happens to one of its members, they know that others will be there to celebrate it with them.

REFLECT

ON THE TEXT

- Where can comparing ourselves to others lead?

- For what reasons might we rejoice at the good
  of the other? What can make joy grow?

- What in this text has touched you the most deeply?

ABOUT MY LIFE

- Why do I sometimes feel a secret joy over evil?
  What, then, rejoices within me?

- What do I find that is good and beautiful
  in my surroundings? In my spouse, in particular?
  How do I try to value it?

- How do I give importance to my spouse's success?

- How do we celebrate, as a couple or as a family,
  something good that happens to one of us?

TO CONCLUDE

- What seems to me important to place
  in the light of Christ to purify it?
  What prayer of thanksgiving do I wish to express?

WITH MY SPOUSE OR IN THE QUIET OF MY HEART,
I want to say: I thank you... I'm sorry... Please...

—

LORD JESUS,
you said, *May my joy be in you and your joy
be complete*. Give us the grace to find our joy
in what is true, what is beautiful, and what is good.

LOVE BEARS ALL THINGS

DOES THE THEME OF THIS SECTION SEEM POSSIBLE TO PUT INTO PRACTICE? HOW SHOULD WE UNDERSTAND IT?

111 Paul's list ends with four phrases containing the words all things. Love bears all things, believes *all things*, hopes all things, endures all things. Here we see clearly the countercultural power of a love that is able to face whatever might threaten it.

112 First, Paul says that love *bears all things* (*panta stégei*). This is about more than simply putting up with evil; it has to do with *the use of the tongue.* The verb can mean "holding one's peace" about what may be wrong with another person. It implies limiting judgment, checking the impulse to issue a firm and ruthless condemnation: *Judge not and you will not be judged* (Lk 6:37). Although it runs contrary to the way we normally use our tongues, God's word tells us: *Do not speak evil against one another, brothers and sisters* (Jas 4:11). Being willing to speak ill of another person is a way of asserting ourselves, venting resentment and envy without concern for the harm we may do. We often forget that slander can be quite sinful; it is a grave offense against God when it seriously harms another person's good name and causes damage that is hard to repair. Hence God's word forthrightly states that the tongue *is a world of iniquity* that *stains the whole body* (Jas 3:6); it is a *restless evil, full of deadly* poison (Jas 3:8). Whereas the tongue can be used to curse those who are made in the likeness of God (Jas 3:9), love cherishes the good name of others, even one's enemies. In seeking to uphold God's law we must never forget this specific requirement of love.

113 Married couples joined by love speak well of each other; they try to show their spouse's good side, not their weakness and faults. In any event, they keep silent rather than speak ill of them. This is not merely a way of acting in front of others; it springs from an interior attitude. Far from ingenuously claiming not to see the problems and weaknesses of others, it sees those weaknesses and faults in a wider context. It recognizes that these failings are a part of a bigger picture. We have to realize that all of us are a complex mixture of light and shadows. The other person is much more than the sum of the little things that annoy me. Love does not have to be perfect for us to value it. The other person loves me as best they can, with all their limits, but the fact that love is imperfect does not mean that it is untrue or unreal. It is real, albeit limited and earthly. If I expect too much, the other person will let me know, for he or she can neither play God nor serve all my needs. Love coexists with imperfection. It *bears all things* and can hold its peace before the limitations of the loved one. ▬

REFLECT

ON THE TEXT

• Why does the pope insist on the word "all"?

• Why is the Gospel so harsh about the "tongue"?

• Why is "'holding one's peace' about what may be wrong with another person" appropriate? In what way is this an act of love?

• What does it mean that "love coexists with imperfection"?

• Which sentences in this section enlighten me, make me wish to grow?

ABOUT MY LIFE

• Do I make an effort to think and speak positively about my spouse?

• To what extent do I take responsibility for my words and the effects they have?

• By what means do I refrain from judging, from arbitrary condemnations at the heart of the family?

• What are my difficulties when faced by the imperfection of the other?

• Am I conscious of the totally extravagant scale of the requirements of love?

TO CONCLUDE

• What simple decision would I like to make to respect my spouse for what he/she is? What request can I make of the Lord?

WITH MY SPOUSE OR IN THE QUIET OF MY HEART,
I want to say: I thank you... I'm sorry... Please...

—

LORD JESUS,
you did not come to condemn the world, but to save it:
teach us to look at one another as you look at us;
guide us to forgive one another as you forgive us.

Complete my joy
by being of the same mind,
with the same love,
united in heart,
thinking one thing.
Do nothing out of selfishness or out of vainglory;
rather, humbly regard others
as more important than yourselves,
each looking out not for his own interests,
but [also] everyone for those of others.

Have among yourselves the same attitude
that is also yours in Christ Jesus,

Who, though he was in the form of God,
did not regard equality with God
something to be grasped.
Rather, he emptied himself,
taking the form of a slave,
coming in human likeness;
and found human in appearance,
he humbled himself,
becoming obedient to death,
even death on a cross.
Because of this, God greatly exalted him
and bestowed on him the name
that is above every name,
that at the name of Jesus
every knee should bend,
of those in heaven and on earth and under the earth,
and every tongue confess that
Jesus Christ is Lord,
to the glory of God the Father.

(Phil 2:2-11)

LOVE BELIEVES ALL THINGS

WHAT DO WE EXPECT FROM TRUST?
WHAT ARE THE ATTITUDES THAT DEMONSTRATE
THAT I HAVE TRUST IN THE OTHER?

114 *Panta pisteúei.* Love believes all things. Here *belief* is not to be taken in its strict theological meaning, but more in the sense of what we mean by "trust." This goes beyond simply presuming that the other is not lying or cheating. Such basic trust recognizes God's light shining beyond the darkness, like an ember glowing beneath the ash.

115 This trust enables a relationship to be free. It means we do not have to control the other person, to follow their every step lest they escape our grip. Love trusts, it sets free, it does not try to control, possess, and dominate everything. This freedom, which fosters independence, an openness to the world around us and to new experiences, can only enrich and expand relationships. The spouses then share with one another the joy of all they have received and learned outside the family circle. At the same time, this freedom makes for sincerity and transparency, for those who know that they are trusted and appreciated can be open and hide nothing. Those who know that their spouse is always suspicious, judgmental, and lacking unconditional love will tend to keep secrets, conceal their failings and weaknesses, and pretend to be someone other than who they are. On the other hand, a family marked by loving trust, come what may, helps its members to be themselves and spontaneously to reject deceit, falsehood, and lies. ▬

LORD, my heart is not proud;
nor are my eyes haughty.
I do not busy myself with great matters,
with things too sublime for me.
Rather, I have stilled my soul,
hushed it like a weaned child.
Like a weaned child on its mother's lap,
so is my soul within me.
Israel, hope in the LORD,
now and forever.

(Psalm 131)

REFLECT

ON THE TEXT

• What terms does the pope use to define trust?

• What counters trust? What are its consequences?

• What impact does trust have on the behavior of another?

ABOUT MY LIFE

• What does the autonomy of each spouse
bring to our marriage?

• How do I show my trust to my spouse?

• In what areas is my trust put to the test?

• The pope notes that trust can be betrayed; what are the
means at my disposal to rebuild trust, come what may?

• Do I encourage my spouse to be open to the world?

TO CONCLUDE

• What prayer would I like to address to the Lord?

• What action would I like to take?

WITH MY SPOUSE OR IN THE QUIET OF MY HEART,
I want to say: I thank you... I'm sorry... Please...

—

LORD,
you tell us that our strength lies in trust:
come bolster the love between us and enliven
our mutual trust, that we may find the energy
needed to go forward together.

LOVE HOPES ALL THINGS

IN WHAT WAY IS HOPE
A PART OF LOVE?

116 *Panta elpízei.* Love does not despair of the future. Following upon what has just been said, this phrase speaks of the hope of one who knows that others can change, mature, and radiate unexpected beauty and untold potential. This does not mean that everything will change in this life. It does involve realizing that, though things may not always turn out as we wish, God may well make crooked lines straight and draw some good from the evil we endure in this world.

117 Here hope comes most fully into its own, for it embraces the certainty of life after death. Each person, with all his or her failings, is called to the fullness of life in heaven. There, fully transformed by Christ's resurrection, every weakness, darkness, and infirmity will pass away. There the person's true being will shine forth in all its goodness and beauty. This realization helps us, amid the aggravations of this present life, to see each person from a supernatural perspective, in the light of hope, and await the fullness that he or she will receive in the heavenly kingdom,* even if it is not yet visible. ▬

REFLECT

ON THE TEXT

• What are the reasons for hope?

• What creates hope of a possible change in the other?

• In what way is a call to hope always present in our failings?

ABOUT MY LIFE

• Am I disappointed when I don't see a change in my spouse? Do I disappoint my spouse by my inability to change certain habits?

• Is my hope linked only to the changes that I expect to see?

• What can I try to change in my life? What can I try to accept in the other?

• How do I perceive the reality of the hereafter and the perfection of the love that will reign there?

• Does my hope take strength from the unconditional love God has for my spouse, for my children, and for me?

TO CONCLUDE

• What prayer can I address to God, that he may make hope grow in me?

WITH MY SPOUSE OR IN THE QUIET OF MY HEART,
I want to say: I thank you... I'm sorry... Please...

—

LORD JESUS,
grant that we may believe that hope does not disappoint,
since your love has been poured into our hearts
by the Holy Spirit who was given to us on the day
of our marriage and on the day of our baptism.

LOVE ENDURES ALL THINGS

DO WE PUT LIMIT ON BEARING EVERY TRIAL? WHAT LIMITS?

118 *Panta hypoménei.* This means that love bears every trial with a positive attitude. It stands firm in hostile surroundings. This *endurance* involves not only the ability to tolerate certain aggravations, but something greater: a constant readiness to confront any challenge. It is a love that *never gives up,* even in the darkest hour. It shows a certain dogged heroism, a power to resist every negative current, an irrepressible commitment to goodness. Here I think of the words of Martin Luther King, who met every kind of trial and tribulation with fraternal love: "The person who hates you most has some good in him;

even the nation that hates you most has some good in it; even the race that hates you most has some good in it. And when you come to the point that you look in the face of every man and see deep down within him what religion calls 'the image of God,' you begin to love him in spite of [everything]. No matter what he does, you see God's image there. There is an element of goodness that he can never slough off.... Another way that you love your enemy is this: when the opportunity presents itself for you to defeat your enemy, that is the time which you must not do it.... When you rise to the level of love, of its great beauty and power, you seek only to defeat evil systems. Individuals who happen to be caught up in that system, you love, but you seek to defeat the system.... Hate for hate only intensifies the existence of hate and evil in the universe. If I hit you and you hit me and I hit you back and you hit me back and so on, you see, that goes on ad infinitum. It just never ends. Somewhere somebody must have a little sense, and that's the strong person. The strong person is the person who can cut off the chain of hate, the chain of evil.... Somebody must have religion enough and morality enough to cut it off and inject within the very structure of the universe that strong and powerful element of love."[11]

119 In family life, we need to cultivate that strength of love which can help us fight every evil threatening it. Love does not yield to resentment, scorn for others, or the desire to hurt or to gain some advantage. The Christian ideal, especially in families, is a love that never gives up. I am sometimes amazed to see men or women who have had to separate from their spouse for their own protection, yet, because of their enduring conjugal love, still try to help them, even by enlisting others, in their moments of illness, suffering, or trial. Here too we see a love that never gives up. ▬

REFLECT

ON THE TEXT

• What do the terms "heroism" and "ideal"
used by the pope evoke in me?

• How does the pope develop what love allows us to endure?
Does this seem to us applicable to the couple and the family?

• What does Martin Luther King's text bring
to the pope's insight?

• What breaks the chain of hate?

• What does the example given by the pope at the end
of this text reveal?

• In what way is "a love that never gives up"
the essence of the Christian ideal?

ABOUT MY LIFE

• Have I ever consciously broken a chain of hate,
a chain of violence?

• Thinking of a particular disagreement with my spouse,
how did we resolve the situation? What part did escalating
verbal abuse, emotional blackmail, recognition and acceptance
of the facts, forgiveness, etc., play?

• Do I feel ready to love to the point of enduring all?

• Am I conscious that, by not responding to the aggression
of the other, I bring gentleness and peace into the world?

TO CONCLUDE

• Before the demands of love, what prayer
do I wish to express today?

WITH MY SPOUSE OR IN THE QUIET OF MY HEART,
I want to say: I thank you... I'm sorry... Please...

—

LORD JESUS,
whose yoke is easy and burden is light, give us the
strength of the Holy Spirit to love, like you, until the end,
and to respond with greater love to what is unbearable.

GROWING
IN CONJUGUAL
LOVE

GROWING IN CONJUGAL LOVE

WHAT DOES THE PHRASE "CONJUGAL CHARITY" REALLY MEAN?
WHAT DOES IT EVOKE FOR ME?

120 Our reflection on Saint Paul's hymn to love has prepared us to discuss conjugal love. This is the love between husband and wife,[12] a love sanctified, enriched, and illuminated by the grace of the sacrament of marriage. It is an "affective union,"[13] spiritual and sacrificial, which combines the warmth of friendship and erotic passion, and endures long after emotions and passion subside. Pope Pius XI taught that this love permeates the duties of married life and enjoys pride of place.[14] Infused by the Holy Spirit, this powerful love is a reflection of the unbroken covenant between Christ and humanity that culminated in his self-sacrifice on the cross. "The Spirit which the Lord pours forth gives a new heart and renders man and woman capable of loving one another as Christ loved us. Conjugal love reaches that fullness to which it is interiorly ordained: conjugal charity."[15]

121 Marriage is a precious sign, for "when a man and a woman celebrate the sacrament of marriage, God is, as it were, 'mirrored' in them; he impresses in them his own features and the indelible character of his love. Marriage is the icon of God's love for us. Indeed, God is also communion: the three

Persons of the Father, the Son, and the Holy Spirit live eternally in perfect unity. And this is precisely the mystery of marriage: God makes of the two spouses one single existence."[16] This has concrete daily consequences, because the spouses, "in virtue of the sacrament, are invested with a true and proper mission, so that, starting with the simple ordinary things of life they can make visible the love with which Christ loves his Church and continues to give his life for her."[17]

122 We should not however confuse different levels: there is no need to lay upon two limited persons the tremendous burden of having to reproduce perfectly the union existing between Christ and his Church, for marriage as a sign entails "a dynamic process…one which advances gradually with the progressive integration of the gifts of God."[18]

> If I speak in human
> and angelic tongues
> but do not have love,
> I am a resounding gong
> or a clashing cymbal.

(1 Cor 13:1)

REFLECT

ON THE TEXT

• What are the links between God and marriage?

• What is the mission of the sacrament of marriage?

• What is my reaction when I read that an affective union
"endures long after emotions and passion subside"?

• What encouragement do I find in these lines?

ABOUT MY LIFE

• Am I conscious of the specific nature of Christian marriage?

• Have I ever experienced the power of this sacrament
in our marriage or witnessed it in others?

• What seems to me capable of damaging,
lessening, or wounding it?

• Am I conscious that the call to perfection
is achieved gradually?

TO CONCLUDE

• Before the grandeur of the sacrament
(and the difficulty of fully living it), what prayer
would I like to address to the God of the covenant?

WITH MY SPOUSE OR IN THE QUIET OF MY HEART,
I want to say: I thank you... I'm sorry... Please...

—

LORD,
you wished for marriage to be in the image of the union
of Christ and the Church: grant us to discover the power
of this great mystery more and more, and to conform to
it with all our heart and all our will.

LIFELONG SHARING

WHAT DOES "TO LIVE TOGETHER" MEAN TO ME?

123 After the love that unites us to God, conjugal love is the "greatest form of friendship."[19] It is a union possessing all the traits of a good friendship: concern for the good of the other, reciprocity, intimacy, warmth, stability, and the resemblance born of a shared life. Marriage joins to all this an indissoluble exclusivity expressed in the stable commitment to share and shape together the whole of life. Let us be honest and acknowledge the signs that this is the case. Lovers do not see their relationship as merely temporary. Those who marry do not expect their excitement to fade. Those who witness the celebration of a loving union, however fragile, trust that it will pass the test of time. Children not only want their parents to love one another, but also to be faithful and remain together. These and similar signs show that it is in the very nature of conjugal love to be definitive. The lasting union expressed by the marriage vows is more than a formality or a traditional formula; it is rooted in the natural inclinations of the human person. For believers, it is also a covenant before God that calls for fidelity: *The Lord was witness to the covenant between you and the wife of your youth, to whom you have been faithless, though she is your companion and your wife by covenant.... Let none be faithless to the wife of his youth. For*

I hate divorce, says the Lord (Mal 2:14-16).

124 A love that is weak or infirm, incapable of accepting marriage as a challenge to be taken up and fought for, reborn, renewed, and reinvented until death, cannot sustain a great commitment. It will succumb to the culture of the ephemeral that prevents a constant process of growth. Yet "promising love for ever is possible when we perceive a plan bigger than our own ideas and undertakings, a plan which sustains us and enables us to surrender our future entirely to the one we love."[20] If this love is to overcome all trials and remain faithful in the face of everything, it needs the gift of grace to strengthen and elevate it. In the words of Saint Robert Bellarmine, "the fact that one man unites with one woman in an indissoluble bond, and that they remain inseparable despite every kind of difficulty, even when there is no longer hope for children, can only be the sign of a great mystery."[21]

125 Marriage is likewise a friendship marked by passion, but a passion always directed to an ever more stable and intense union. This is because "marriage was not instituted solely for the procreation of children" but also that mutual love "might be properly expressed, that it should grow and mature."[22] This unique friendship between a man and a woman acquires an all-encompassing character only within the conjugal union. Precisely as all-encompassing, this union is also exclusive, faithful, and open to new life. It shares everything in constant mutual respect. The Second Vatican

JOY AND BEAUTY

WHAT DO THESE TWO WORDS EVOKE WHEN WE THINK ABOUT CONJUGAL LOVE?

126 In marriage, the joy of love needs to be cultivated. When the search for pleasure becomes obsessive, it holds us in thrall and keeps us from experiencing other satisfactions. Joy, on the other hand, increases our pleasure and helps us find fulfilment in any number of things, even at those times of life when physical pleasure has ebbed. Saint Thomas Aquinas said that the word "joy" refers to an expansion of the heart.[24] Marital joy can be experienced even amid sorrow; it involves accepting that marriage is an inevitable mixture of enjoyment and struggles, tensions and repose, pain and relief, satisfactions and longings, annoyances and plea-

sures, but always on the path of friendship, which inspires married couples to care for one another: "they help and serve each other."[25]

127 The love of friendship is called "charity" when it perceives and esteems the "great worth" of another person.[26] Beauty— that "great worth" which is other than physical or psychological appeal enables us to appreciate the sacredness of a person, without feeling the need to possess it. In a consumerist society, the sense of beauty is impoverished and so joy fades. Everything is there to be purchased, possessed, or consumed, including people. Tenderness, on the other

Be subordinate to one another
out of reverence for Christ.
As the Church is subordinate to Christ,
so wives should be subordinate
to their husbands in everything.
Husbands, love your wives,
even as Christ loved the church
and handed himself over for her.
So [also] husbands should love their wives
as their own bodies.
He who loves his wife loves himself.
For no one hates his own flesh
but rather nourishes and cherishes it,
even as Christ does the church,
because we are members of his body.

"For this reason a man shall leave [his] father
    and [his] mother
and be joined to his wife,
and the two shall become one flesh."

This is a great mystery,
but I speak in reference to Christ and the church.
In any case,
each one of you should love his wife as himself,
and the wife should respect her husband.

(Eph 5:21, 24-25, 28-33)

PASSIONATE LOVE

HOW WOULD I DEFINE THE CHARACTERISTICS OF THE SACRAMENT OF MARRIAGE?

142 The Second Vatican Council teaches that this conjugal love "embraces the good of the whole person; it can enrich the sentiments of the spirit and their physical expression with a unique dignity and ennoble them as the special features and manifestation of the friendship proper to marriage."[35] For this reason, a love lacking either pleasure or passion is insufficient to symbolize the union of the human heart with God: "All the mystics have affirmed that supernatural love and heavenly love find the symbols which they seek in marital love, rather than in friendship, filial devotion, or devotion to a cause. And the reason is to be found precisely in its totality."[36] Why then should we not pause to speak of feelings and sexuality in marriage? ■

Eat, friends, drink!
For stern as death is love,
relentless as the nether world is devotion;
its flames are a blazing fire. 🙶

(Song 5:1; 8:6)

In this brief section, Pope Francis introduces the following part of his text by noting that, if the mystics drew their spiritual metaphors from human love, it is because conjugal love represents the totality of love.

This extract from *The Living Flame of Love* by Saint John of the Cross is an example of this.

How gently and lovingly
You wake in my heart,
Where in secret you dwell alone;
And in your sweet breathing,
Filled with good and glory,
How tenderly you swell my heart with love.
(Stanza 4)

THE WORLD OF EMOTIONS

WHAT DOES THE TITLE
OF THIS SECTION EVOKE FOR ME?

143 Desires, feelings, emotions, what the ancients called "the passions," all have an important place in married life. They are awakened whenever "another" becomes present and part of a person's life. It is characteristic of all living beings to reach out to other things, and this tendency always has basic affective signs: pleasure or pain, joy or sadness, tenderness or fear. They ground the most elementary psychological activity. Human beings live on this earth, and all that they do and seek is fraught with passion.

144 As true man, Jesus showed his emotions. He was hurt by the rejection of Jerusalem (cf. Mt 23:27) and this moved him to tears (cf. Lk 19:41). He was also deeply moved by the sufferings of others (cf. Mk 6:34). He felt deeply their grief (cf. Jn 11:33), and he wept at the death of a friend (cf. Jn 11:35). These examples of his sensitivity showed how much his human heart was open to others.

145 Experiencing an emotion is not, in itself, morally good or evil.[37] The stirring of desire or repugnance is neither sinful nor blameworthy. What is morally good or evil is what we do on the basis of, or under the influence of, a given passion. But when passions are aroused or sought, and as a result we perform evil acts, the evil lies in the decision to fuel them and in the evil acts that result. Along the same lines, my being attracted to someone is not automatically good. If my attraction to that person makes me try to dominate him or her, then my feeling only serves my selfishness. To believe that we are good simply because "we feel good" is a tremendous illusion. There are those who feel themselves capable of great love only because they have a great need for affection, yet they prove incapable of the effort needed to bring happiness to others. They remain caught up in their own needs and desires. In such cases, emotions distract from the highest values and conceal a self-centeredness that makes it impossible to develop a healthy and happy family life.

146 This being said, if passion accompanies a free act, it can manifest the depth of that act. Marital love strives to ensure that one's entire emotional life benefits the family as a whole and stands at the service of its common life. A family is mature when the emotional life of its members becomes a form of sensitivity that neither stifles nor obscures great decisions and values, but rather follows each one's freedom,[38] springs from it, enriches, perfects, and harmonizes it in the service of all. ▬

REFLECT

ON THE TEXT

- What is the place and role of emotion in human life?

- The Gospel shows us Jesus gripped by emotions:
  which ones?

- Do emotions and feelings have a moral value?
  What's more important: the emotions or the steps
  I take with regard to them?

- What are the obstacles to a stimulating emotional life?

ABOUT MY LIFE

- How do I manage my emotions? Do I let them guide me
  or do I master them? And to what end?

- What is the place of sensitivity in my life
  as a couple and as a family?

- Do I nurse negative emotions that push me
  to make decisions contrary to real love?

- Am I conscious of emotions that have led me to do good?

- Do I perceive in myself emotions that help me
  to be at the service of my spouse?

TO CONCLUDE

- What prayer would I like to address to God,
  who has given me emotional sensitivity for my good
  and the good of my neighbor?

WITH MY SPOUSE OR IN THE QUIET OF MY HEART,
I want to say: I thank you... I'm sorry... Please...

—

LORD JESUS,
when you were seized by compassion, your love reached
out to others in tenderness; grant us to understand the
value of emotions that bring us to love our neighbors,
our friends, and even our enemies with a renewed love.

Hark! my lover—here he comes
springing across the mountains,
leaping across the hills.
My lover is like a gazelle
or a young stag.
Here he stands behind our wall,
gazing through the windows,
peering through the lattices.
My lover speaks; he says to me,
"Arise, my beloved, my beautiful one,
and come!

"The fig tree puts forth its figs,
and the vines, in bloom, give forth fragrance.
Arise, my beloved, my beautiful one, and come!

"O my dove in the clefts of the rock,
in the secret recesses of the cliff,
Let me see you,
let me hear your voice,
For your voice is sweet,
and you are lovely."

My lover belongs to me and I to him;
he browses among the lilies.

Set me as a seal on your heart,
as a seal on your arm;
For stern as death is love,
relentless as the nether world is devotion;
its flames are a blazing fire.
Deep waters cannot quench love,
nor floods sweep it away.
Were one to offer all he owns to purchase love,
he would be roundly mocked.

(Song 2:8-10, 13-14, 16; 8:6-7)

GOD LOVES THE JOY OF HIS CHILDREN

WHAT DOES THE TITLE OF THIS SECTION MAKE ME THINK OF?

147 This calls for a pedagogical process that involves renunciation. This conviction on the part of the Church has often been rejected as opposed to human happiness. Benedict XVI summed up this charge with great clarity: "Doesn't the Church, with all her commandments and prohibitions, turn to bitterness the most precious thing in life? Doesn't she blow the whistle just when the joy which is the Creator's gift offers us a happiness which is itself a certain foretaste of the Divine?"[39] He responded that, although there have been exaggerations and deviant forms of asceticism in Christianity, the Church's official teaching, in fidelity to the Scriptures,* did not reject "*eros* as such, but rather declared war on a warped and destructive form of it, because this counterfeit divinization of *eros*…actually strips it of divine dignity and dehumanizes it."[40]

148 Training in the areas of emotion and instinct is necessary, and at times this requires setting limits. Excess, lack of control, or obsession with a single form of pleasure can end up weakening and tainting that very pleasure[41] and damaging family life. A person can certainly channel his passions in a beautiful and healthy way, increasingly pointing them towards altruism and an integrated self-fulfillment that can only enrich interpersonal relationships in the heart of the family. This does not mean renouncing moments of intense enjoyment,[42] but rather integrating them with other moments of generous commitment, patient hope, inevitable weariness, and struggle to achieve an ideal. Family life is all this, and it deserves to be lived to the fullest.

149 Some currents of spirituality teach that desire has to be eliminated as a path to liberation from pain. Yet we believe that God loves the enjoyment felt by human beings: he created us and *richly furnishes us with everything to enjoy* (1 Tm 6:17). Let us be glad when with great love he tells us: *My son, treat yourself well…. Do not deprive yourself of a happy day*

(Sir 14:11-14). Married couples likewise respond to God's will when they take up the biblical injunction: *Be joyful in the day of prosperity* (Eccl 7:14). What is important is to have the freedom to realize that pleasure can find different expressions at different times of life, in accordance with the needs of mutual love. In this sense, we can appreciate the teachings of some Eastern masters who urge us to expand our consciousness, lest we be imprisoned by one limited experience that can blinker us. This expansion of consciousness is not the denial or destruction of desire so much as its broadening and perfection. ▬

REFLECT

ON THE TEXT

• What do I discover in these lines?
What seems most important to me?

• Do the pope's words reassure me? Challenge me?

• Why must we work to control our emotions
and instincts?

• What are the various forms of love
that enrich common life?

ABOUT MY LIFE

• Does Church teaching strike me as a constraint
that I reject? Do I seek to understand this teaching to know
what it really proposes? Do I believe that this teaching
can lead me to happiness?

• Does renunciation have meaning for me?
How can I express it?

• In what concrete ways do we express our love?

• What moments of happiness experienced in our life
as a couple give us a foretaste of something divine?

TO CONCLUDE

• Drawing on the range of the expressions of love,
what prayer can I address to God?

WITH MY SPOUSE OR IN THE QUIET OF MY HEART,
I want to say: I thank you... I'm sorry... Please...

—

LORD JESUS,
you reveal to us your inexhaustible mercy;
pour your grace upon us, that we may love as you love,
with an undivided heart, attentive and inventive,
ceaselessly seeking the good of the other,
their joy and their happiness.

THE EROTIC DIMENSION OF LOVE

HOW DO YOU REACT TO THE TITLE OF THIS SECTION?
DO WE THINK THE CHURCH HAS ANYTHING TO TELL US
ABOUT THE EROTIC DIMENSION OF LOVE?

150 All this brings us to the sexual dimension of marriage. God himself created sexuality, which is a marvelous gift to his creatures. If this gift needs to be cultivated and directed, it is to prevent the "impoverishment of an authentic value."[43] Saint John Paul II rejected the claim that the Church's teaching is "a negation of the value of human sexuality," or that the Church simply tolerates sexuality "because it is necessary for procreation."[44] Sexual desire is not something to be looked down upon, and "and there can be no attempt whatsoever to call into question its necessity."[45]

151 To those who fear that the training of the passions and of sexuality detracts from the spontaneity of sexual love, Saint John Paul II replied that human persons are "called to full and mature spontaneity in their relationships," a maturity that "is the gradual fruit of a discernment of the impulses of one's own heart."[46] This calls for discipline and self-mastery, since every human person "must learn, with perseverance and consistency, the meaning of his or her body."[47] Sexuality is not a means of gratification or entertainment; it is an interpersonal language wherein the other is taken seriously, in his or her sacred and inviolable dignity. As such, "the human heart comes to participate, so to speak, in another kind of spontaneity."[48] In this context, the erotic appears as a specifically human manifestation of sexuality. It enables us to discover "the nuptial meaning of the body and the authentic dignity of the gift."[49] In his catecheses on the theology of the body, Saint John Paul II taught that sexual differentiation not only is "a source of fruitfulness and procreation," but also possesses "the capacity of expressing love: that love precisely in which the human person becomes a gift."[50] A healthy sexual desire, albeit closely joined to a pursuit of pleasure, always involves a sense of wonder, and for that very reason can humanize the impulses.

152 In no way, then, can we consider the erotic dimension of love simply as a permissible evil or a burden to be tolerated for the good of the family. Rather, it must be seen as gift from God that enriches the relationship of the spouses. As a passion sublimated by a love respectful of the dignity of the other, it becomes a "pure, unadulterated affirmation" revealing the marvels of which the human heart is capable. In this way, even momentarily, we can feel that "life has turned out good and happy."[51] ▬

REFLECT

ON THE TEXT

• What draws my attention? What do I discover?

• Why does the pope insist upon the "dignity of the other"?
In what way is this important
for the erotic dimension of love?

ABOUT MY LIFE

• How do I react before the different components
of sexuality: eroticism, pleasure, personal satisfaction,
body language, reciprocal expressions of love, wonder
before the other, forms of gift of self to the other,
spontaneity, etc.?

• Am I conscious that the language of the bodies is a form
of dialogue, a kind of communication between persons
that is learned and perfected over time?

TO CONCLUDE

• How can we praise God for the beauty
of human sexuality?

WITH MY SPOUSE OR IN THE QUIET OF MY HEART,
I want to say: I thank you... I'm sorry... Please...

—

LORD OUR GOD,
may your Spirit reveal to us the beauty of love, including
its erotic dimension; keep us from damaging what,
since the creation of man and woman, is "very good";
and grant us to live in the wonder and the joy of this
reciprocal gift of self.

VIOLENCE
AND MANIPULATION

DOES THE SUBJECT OF THIS SECTION SEEM TO US
CONSISTENT WITH THE PRECEDING SECTION?
IN WHAT SENSE DO WE UNDERSTAND IT?

153 On the basis of this positive vision of sexuality, we can approach the entire subject with a healthy realism. It is, after all, a fact that sex often becomes depersonalized and unhealthy; as a result, "it becomes the occasion and instrument for self-assertion and the selfish satisfaction of personal desires and instincts."[52] In our own day, sexuality risks being poisoned by the mentality of "use and discard." The body of the other is often viewed as an object to be used as long as it offers satisfaction, and rejected once it is no longer appealing. Can we really ignore or overlook the continuing forms of domination, arrogance, abuse, sexual perversion, and violence that are the product of a warped understanding of sexuality? Or the fact that the dignity of others and our human vocation to love thus end up being less important than an obscure need to "find oneself"?

154 We also know that, within marriage itself, sex can become a source of suffering and manipulation. Hence it must be clearly reaffirmed that "a conjugal act imposed on one's spouse without regard to his or her condition, or personal and reasonable wishes in the matter, is no true act of love, and therefore offends the moral order in its particular application to the intimate relationship of husband and wife."[53] The acts proper to the sexual union of husband and wife correspond to the nature of sexuality as willed by God when they take place in "a manner which is truly human.[54] Saint Paul insists: *Let no one transgress and wrong his brother or sister in this matter* (1 Thes 4:6). Even though Paul was writing in the context of a patriarchal culture in which women were considered completely subordinate to men, he nonetheless taught that sex must involve communication between the spouses: he brings up the possibility of postponing sexual relations for a period, but *by agreement* (1 Cor 7:5).

155 Saint John Paul II very subtly warned that a couple can be "threatened by insatiability."[55] In other words, while called to an increasingly profound union, they can risk effacing their differences and the rightful distance between the two. For each possesses his or her own proper and inalienable dignity. When reciprocal belonging turns into domination, "the structure of communion in interpersonal relations is essentially changed."[56] It is part of the mentality of domination that those who dominate end up negating their own dignity.[57] Ultimately, they no longer "identify themselves subjectively with their own body,"[58] because they take away its deepest meaning. They end up using sex as form of escapism and renounce the beauty of conjugal union.

156 Every form of sexual submission must be clearly rejected. This includes all improper interpretations of the passage in the Letter to the Ephesians where Paul tells women to *be subject to your husbands* (Eph 5:22). This passage mirrors the cultural categories of the time, but our concern is not with its cultural matrix but with the revealed message that it conveys. As Saint John Paul II wisely observed: "Love excludes every kind of subjection whereby the wife might become a servant or a slave of the husband…. The community or unity which they should establish through marriage is constituted by a reciprocal donation of self, which is also a mutual subjection."[59] Hence Paul goes on to say that *husbands should love their wives as their own bodies* (Eph 5:28). The biblical text is actually concerned with encouraging everyone to overcome a complacent individualism and to be constantly mindful of others: *Be subject to one another* (Eph 5:21). In marriage, this reciprocal "submission" takes on a special meaning, and is seen as a freely chosen mutual belonging marked by fidelity, respect, and care. Sexuality is inseparably at the service of this conjugal friendship, for it is meant to aid the fulfilment of the other.

157 All the same, the rejection of distortions of sexuality and eroticism should never lead us to a disparagement or neglect of sexuality and *eros* in themselves. The ideal of marriage cannot be seen purely as generous donation and self-sacrifice, where each spouse renounces all personal needs and seeks only the other's good without concern for personal satisfaction. We need to remember that authentic love also needs to be able to receive the other, to accept one's own vulnerability and needs, and to welcome with sincere and joyful gratitude the physical expressions of love found in a caress, an embrace, a kiss, and sexual union. Benedict XVI stated this very clearly: "Should man aspire to be pure spirit and to reject the flesh as pertaining to his animal nature alone, then spirit and body would both lose their dignity."[60] For this reason, "man cannot live by oblative, descending love alone. He cannot always give, he must also receive. Anyone who wishes to give love must also receive love as a gift."[61] Still, we must never forget that our human equilibrium is fragile; there is a part of us that resists real human growth, and any moment it can unleash the most primitive and selfish tendencies. =

There is no fear in love, but perfect love drives out fear because fear has to do with punishment, and so one who fears is not yet perfect in love.

We love because he first loved us.

(1 Jn 4:18-19)

REFLECT

ON THE TEXT

• What do we discover in this long text? What holds our attention? What disconcerts us? What clarifications do we notice in comparison to the preceding section?

• What are the two inseparable and indispensable conditions for well-balanced love?

• How do John Paul II and Benedict XVI view sexuality?

ABOUT MY LIFE

• Am I sometimes aware that I'm using my spouse for my own satisfaction?

• How does the sexual act in our marriage figure at the heart of dialogue? How do we address the question of our own availability to it?

• How do I put faithfulness, respect, and care into practice?

• How do I consider that a conjugal sexual relationship combines entitlement and gift?

• Am I aware, for myself and my spouse, of the need to give and the need to receive?

TO CONCLUDE

• In response to the grandeur and the difficulties of sexuality, which prayers do I wish to express?

WITH MY SPOUSE OR IN THE QUIET OF MY HEART,
I want to say: I thank you... I'm sorry... Please...

—

LORD,
You desired that man and woman live a marvelous,
reciprocal belonging in the union of body, soul, and spirit;
teach us to be deferential to one another in love,
knowing how to give as much as to receive.

MARRIAGE AND VIRGINITY

IN WHAT WAY DO THESE TWO STATES OF LIFE SEEM IMPORTANT TO ME?

158 "Many people who are unmarried are not only devoted to their own family but often render great service in their group of friends, in the Church community, and in their professional lives. Sometimes their presence and contributions are overlooked, causing in them a sense of isolation. Many put their talents at the service of the Christian community through charity and volunteer work. Others remain unmarried because they consecrate their lives to the love of Christ and neighbor. Their dedication greatly enriches the family, the Church, and society."[62]

159 Virginity is a form of love. As a sign, it speaks to us of the coming of the Kingdom and the need for complete devotion to the cause of the Gospel (cf. 1 Cor 7:32). It is also a reflection of the fullness of heaven, *where they neither marry not are given in marriage* (Mt 22:30). Saint Paul recommended virginity because he expected Jesus' imminent return and he wanted everyone to concentrate only on spreading the Gospel: *the appointed time has grown very short* (1 Cor 7:29). Nonetheless, he made it clear that this was his personal opinion and preference (cf. 1 Cor 7:6-9), not something demanded by Christ: *I have no command in the Lord* (1 Cor 7:25). All the same, he recognized the value of the different callings: *Each has his or her own special gift from God, one of one kind and one of another* (1 Cor 7:7). Reflecting on this, Saint John Paul II noted that the biblical texts "give no reason to assert the 'inferiority' of marriage, nor the 'superiority' of virginity or celibacy"[63] based on sexual abstinence. Rather than speak absolutely of the superiority of virginity, it should be enough to point out that the different states of life complement one another, and consequently that some can be more perfect in one way and others in another. Alexander of Hales, for example, stated that in one sense marriage may be considered superior to the other sacraments, inasmuch as it symbolizes the great reality of "Christ's union with the Church, or the union of his divine and human natures."[64]

160 Consequently, "it is not a matter of diminishing the value of matrimony in favor of continence."[65] "There is no basis for playing one off against the other…. If, following a certain theological tradition, one speaks of a 'state of perfection' (*status perfectionis*), this has to do not with continence in itself, but with the entirety of a life based on the evangelical counsels."[66] A married person can experience the highest degree of charity and thus "reach the perfection which flows from charity, through fidelity to the spirit of those counsels. Such perfection is possible and accessible to every man and woman."[67]

161 The value of virginity lies in its symbolizing a love that has no need to possess the other; in this way it reflects the freedom of the Kingdom of heaven. Virginity encourages married couples to live their own conjugal love against the backdrop of Christ's definitive love, journeying together towards the fullness of the kingdom. For its part, conjugal love symbolizes other values. On the one hand, it is a particular reflection of that full unity in distinction found in the Trinity. The family is also a sign of Christ. It manifests the closeness of God who is a part of every human life, since he became one with us through his Incarnation, Death, and Resurrection. Each spouse becomes "one flesh" with the other as a sign of willingness to share everything with him or her until death. Whereas virginity is an "eschatological"* sign of the Risen Christ, marriage is a "historical" sign for us living in this world, a sign of the earthly Christ who chose to become one with us and gave himself up for us even to shedding his

blood. Virginity and marriage are, and must be, different ways of loving. For "man cannot live without love. He remains a being that is incomprehensible for himself; his life is senseless, if love is not revealed to him." [68]

162 Celibacy* can risk becoming a comfortable single life that provides the freedom to be independent, to move from one residence, work, or option to another, to spend money as one sees fit and to spend time with others as one wants. In such cases, the witness of married people becomes especially eloquent. Those called to virginity can encounter in some marriages a clear sign of God's generous and steadfast fidelity to his covenant, and this can move them to a more concrete and generous availability to others. Many married couples remain faithful when one of them has become physically unattractive, or fails to satisfy the other's needs, despite the voices in our society that might encourage them to be unfaithful or to leave the other. A wife can care for her sick husband and thus, in drawing near to the cross, renew her commitment to love unto death. In such love, the dignity of the true lover shines forth, inasmuch as it is more proper to charity to love than to be loved.[69] We could also point to the presence in many families of a capacity for selfless and loving service when children prove troublesome and even ungrateful. This makes those parents a sign of the free and selfless love of Jesus. Cases like these encourage celibate persons to live their commitment to the kingdom with greater generosity and openness. Today, secularization* has obscured the value of a lifelong union and the beauty of the vocation to marriage. For this reason, it is "necessary to deepen an understanding of the *positive* aspects of conjugal love."[70]

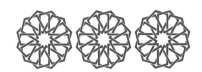

REFLECT

ON THE TEXT

• Which sentences stand out for me?
What have I discovered?

• What connections are there between
marriage and virginity?

• What can celibate life learn from married life?

• In what ways are marriage and virginity
different manners of loving?
In what ways are they complementary?

ABOUT MY LIFE

• Do I know consecrated people,
people who have chosen a life of celibacy?
Do I ever talk with them about the richness
of our vocations?

• How does their witness teach me
something about my life as a spouse?

• Have I ever had occasion to see that my marriage
and my family life are, for others, a witness
of disinterested love?

TO CONCLUDE

• What prayer do I wish to address to God,
who fulfills each one of his children?

WITH MY SPOUSE OR IN THE QUIET OF MY HEART,
I want to say: I thank you... I'm sorry... Please...

—

LORD,
you grant that each of us, according to our vocation,
may find you by offering ourselves: make us ever more
open to your grace and faithful to our vows.

THE TRANSFORMATION OF LOVE

HOW DO WE SEE LOVE TRANSFORM ITSELF OVER THE COURSE OF OUR RELATIONSHIP?

163 Longer life spans now mean that close and exclusive relationships must last for four, five, or even six decades; consequently, the initial decision has to be frequently renewed. While one of the spouses may no longer experience an intense sexual desire for the other, he or she may still experience the pleasure of mutual belonging and the knowledge that neither of them is alone but has a "partner" with whom everything in life is shared. He or she is a companion on life's journey, one with whom to face life's difficulties and enjoy its pleasures. This satisfaction is part of the affection proper to conjugal love. There is no guarantee that we will feel the same way all through life. Yet if a couple can come up with a shared and lasting life project, they can love one another and live as one until death do them part, enjoying an enriching intimacy. The love they pledge is greater than any emotion, feeling, or state of mind, although it may include all of these. It is a deeper love, a lifelong decision of the heart. Even amid unresolved conflicts and confused emotional situations, they daily reaffirm their decision to love, to belong to one another, to share their lives, and to continue loving and forgiving. Each progresses along the path of personal growth and development. On this journey, love rejoices at every step and in every new stage.

164 In the course of every marriage physical appearances change, but this hardly means that love and attraction need fade. We love the other person for who they are, not simply for their body. Although the body ages, it still expresses that personal identity that first won our heart. Even if others can no longer see the beauty of that identity, a spouse continues to see it with the eyes of love and so his or her affection does not diminish. He or she reaffirms the decision to belong to the other and expresses that choice in faithful and loving closeness. The nobility of this decision, by its intensity and depth, gives rise to a new kind of emotion as they fulfil their marital mission. For "emotion, caused by another human being as a person…does not *per se* tend toward the conjugal act."[71] It finds other sensible expressions. Indeed, love "is a single reality, but with different dimensions; at different times, one or other dimension may emerge more clearly."[72] The marriage bond finds new forms of expression and constantly seeks new ways to grow in strength. These both preserve and strengthen the bond. They call for daily effort. None of this, however, is possible without praying to the Holy Spirit for an outpouring of his grace, his supernatural strength, and his spiritual fire, to confirm, direct, and transform our love in every new situation. ▬

""

Unless a grain
of wheat falls
to the ground
and dies, it remains
just a grain of wheat;
but if it dies,
it produces much fruit. **""**

(Jn 12:24)

REFLECT

ON THE TEXT

- What do I take away from this last section?

- What does the pope mean when he speaks of love as a daily decision, or when he says that "the decision has to be frequently renewed"?

- What is the pope trying to make us understand in this section?

- What are the means he proposes?

ABOUT MY LIFE

- On several occasions, the pope uses the word decision. Do I recall, as a couple, having felt that love is also a question of a decision?

- In what way do the pope's words seem to me meaningful to us as a couple? Does it seem to me a warning about the long-term?

- How do I build this future starting today?

- What is for us the "shared and lasting life project" of which the pope speaks?

TO CONCLUDE

- Prayer is at the heart of the life of a couple and its growth; what prayer can I address to God so our love as a couple grows?

WITH MY SPOUSE OR IN THE QUIET OF MY HEART,
I want to say: I thank you... I'm sorry... Please...

—

SEND YOUR SPIRIT, O LORD,
to renew the face of the earth; you know our
weaknesses, but since all our hope is in you, we dare
to ask for faithfulness in love, for strength in adversity,
and for the joy to advance together in your sight.

Do to others as you would have them do to you.
For if you love those who love you,
what credit is that to you?
Even sinners love those who love them.

And if you do good to those who do good to you,
what credit is that to you?
Even sinners do the same.

If you lend money
to those from whom you expect repayment,
what credit [is] that to you?
Even sinners lend to sinners,
and get back the same amount.

But rather,
love your enemies and do good to them,
and lend expecting nothing back;
then your reward will be great
and you will be children of the Most High,
for he himself is kind to the ungrateful
and the wicked.

Be merciful,
just as [also] your Father is merciful.

Stop judging and you will not be judged.
Stop condemning and you will not be condemned.
Forgive and you will be forgiven.

Give and gifts will be given to you;
a good measure, packed together,
shaken down, and overflowing,
will be poured into your lap.
For the measure with which you measure
will in return be measured out to you.

(Lk 6:31-38)

APPENDIX

NOTES

1. *Catechism of the Catholic Church,* 1641.

2. Cf. Benedict XVI, Encyclical Letter *Deus caritas est* (December 25, 2005), 2: AAS 98 (2006), 218.

3. *Spiritual Exercises,* "Contemplation to Attain Love" (230).

4. Octavio Paz, *La llama doble* (Barcelona: Seix Barral, 1993), 35.

5. Thomas Aquinas, *Summa theologiae* II-II, q. 114, art. 2, ad. 1.

6. Benedict XVI, Catechesis (May 13, 2005): *L'Osservatore Romano,* May 14, 2015, p. 8.

7. *Summa theologiae,* II-II, q. 27, art. 1, ad. 2.

8. *Summa theologiae,* II-II, q. 27, art. 1.

9. Francis, Catechesis (May 13, 2015): *L'Osservatore Romano,* May 14, 2015, p. 8.

10. John Paul II, Apostolic Exhortation *Familiaris consortio* (November 22, 1981), 21: AAS 74 (1982), 106.

11. Martin Luther King Jr., "Sermon delivered at Dexter Avenue Baptist Church" (Montgomery, Alabama, November 17, 1957).

12. Thomas Aquinas calls love a *vis unitiva* (ST I, q. 20, art. 1, ad. 3), echoing a phrase of Pseudo-Dionysius the Areopagite (*De Divinis Nominibus,* IV, 12: PG 3, 709).

13. ST II-II, q. 27, art. 2.

14. Pius XI, Encyclical Letter *Casti connubii* (December 31, 1930): AAS 22 (1930), 547–548.

15. *Familiaris Consortio,* 13.

16. Francis, Catechesis (April 2, 2014): *L'Osservatore Romano,* April 3, 2014, p. 8.

17. *Ibid.*

18. *Familiaris Consortio,* 9.

19. Thomas Aquinas, *Summa contra Gentiles* III, 123; cf. Aristotle, *Nicomachean Ethics,* 8, 12 (Oxford: Bywater, 1984), 174.

20. Francis, Encyclical Letter *Lumen Fidei* (June 29, 2013), 52: AAS 105 (2013), 590.

21. De *sacramento matrimonii,* I, 2; in Id., *Disputationes,* III, 5, 3 (ed. Giuliano, Naples, 1858), 778.

22. Second Vatican Council, Pastoral Constitution *Gaudium et* *spes* (December 7, 1965), 50.

23. *Gaudium et spes.*, 49.

24. Cf. ST I-II, q. 31, art. 3., ad. 3.

25. *Gaudium et spes,* 48.

26. Cf. ST I-II, q. 26, art. 3.

27. ST q. 110, art. 1.

28. Augustine, *Confessions*, VIII, III, 7: PL 32, 752.

29. Francis, Address to the Pilgrimage of Families during the Year of Faith (October 26, 2013): AAS 105 (2013), 980.

30. Francis, Angelus Message (December 29, 2013): *L'Osservatore Romano*, December 30-31, 2013, p. 7.

31. Francis, Address to the Pilgrimage of Families during the Year of Faith (October 26, 2013): AAS 105 (2013), 978.

32. ST II-II, q. 24, art. 7.

33. *Gaudium et spes,* 48.

34. Chilean Bishops' Conference, *La vida y la familia: regalos de Dios para cada uno de nosotros* (July 21, 2014).

35. *Gaudium et spes,* 49.

36. Antonin Gilbert Sertillanges, *L'Amour chrétien* (Paris: Lecoffre, 1920), 174.

37. Cf. ST I-II, q. 24, art. 1.

38. Cf. ST q. 59, art. 5.

39. *Deus caritas est,* 3.

40. *Deus caritas est,* 4.

41. Cf. ST I-II, q. 32, art.7.

42. Cf. ST II-II, q. 153, art. 2, ad. 2: *Abundantia delectationis quae est in actu venereo secundum rationem ordinato, non contrariatur medio virtutis.*

43. John Paul II, Catechesis (October 22, 1980), 5: *Insegnamenti* III/2 (1980), 951.

44. *Ibid.,* 3.

45. John Paul II, Catechesis, (September 24, 1980), 4: *Insegnamenti* III/2 (1980), 719.

46. John Paul II, Catechesis (November 12, 1980), 2: *Insegnamenti* III/2 (1980), 1133.

47. *Ibid.,* 4.

48. *Ibid.,* 5.

49. *Ibid.,* 1: 1132.

50. John Paul II, Catechesis (January 16, 1980), 1: *Insegnamenti* III/1 (1980), 151.

51. Josef Pieper, *Über die Liebe*

(Munich: Kösel-Verlag, 2014), 174. English: *On Love*, in *Faith, Hope, Love* (San Francisco: Ignatius Press, 1997), 256.

52. John Paul II, Encyclical Letter *Evangelium vitae* (March 25, 1995), 23: AAS 87 (1995), 427.

53. Paul VI, Encyclical Letter *Humanae vitae* (July 25, 1968), 13: AAS 60 (1968), 489.

54. *Gaudium et spes*, 49.

55. John Paul II, Catechesis (June 18, 1980), 5: *Insegnamenti* III/1 (1980), 1778.

56. *Ibid.*, 6.

57. Cf. Catechesis (July 30, 1980), 1: *Insegnamenti* III/2 (1980), 311.

58. Catechesis (April 8, 1981), 3: *Insegnamenti* IV/1 (1981), 904.

59. Catechesis (August 11, 1982), 4: *Insegnamenti* V/3 (1982), 205-206.

60. *Deus caritas est*, 5.

61. *Deus caritas est*, 7.

62. Synod of Bishops, XIV Ordinary General Assembly: The Vocation and Mission of the Family in the Church and in the Contemporary World, *Relatio finalis* (October 24, 2015), 22.

63. John Paul II, Catechesis (April 14, 1982), 1: *Insegnamenti* V/1 (1982), 1176.

64. *Glossa in quatuor libros sententiarum Petri Lombardi*, IV, XXVI, 2 (Quaracchi, 1957, 446).

65. John Paul II, Catechesis (April 7, 1982), 2: *Insegnamenti* V/1 (1982), 1127.

66. John Paul II, Catechesis (April 14, 1982), 3: *Insegnamenti* V/1 (1982), 1177.

67. *Ibid.*

68. John Paul II, Encyclical Letter *Redemptor hominis* (March 4, 1979), 10: AAS 71 (1979), 274.

69. Cf. ST II-II, q. 27, art. 1.

70. Pontifical Council for the Family, *Family, Marriage and "De Facto" Unions* (July 26, 2000), 40.

71. John Paul II, Catechesis (October 31, 1984), 6: *Insegnamenti* VII/2 (1984), 1072.

72. *Deus caritas est*, 8.

GLOSSARY

Apostolic Exhortation: A text issued by the pope following a synod,* primarily addressed to the Catholic bishops of the world.

Book of Wisdom: Book of the Old Testament.

Celibacy: Long-term or temporary sexual abstinence, not to be confused with chastity, which is the refusal to consider a person as an object for one's own personal satisfaction.

Charity: Unconditional, freely given love that seeks the good of the beloved.

Covenant: A central concept of the Bible, it refers to the nature of the relationship God wished to establish with humanity.

Eschatological: A term for all things concerning the end of the world.

Law of God: In the pope's text, this term refers to the Decalogue, also known as the Ten Commandments.

Family apostolate: A service of the Church aimed at supporting the life of Christian families and their members.

Kingdom of God (or of heaven): Refers to both the divine world to which God calls us and his unique manner of reigning through love.

Mercy: An attribute of God explaining his entire plan for the salvation of humanity, characterized by a disposition of loving pardon, sensitivity to the poverty and suffering of others, and a fundamental benevolence toward others.

Sacrament: The sign and means of communion with God and between men. There are seven sacraments: baptism, Eucharist, confirmation, confession (reconciliation), anointing of the sick, holy orders (when one becomes a deacon, priest, or bishop), and, of course, marriage.

Scripture: Another term for the Bible, which is comprised of the 73 books of the Old and New Testaments.

Second Vatican Council: The assembly of Catholic bishops worldwide held at the Vatican from 1962 to 1965 to, together, update the role of the Church and its mission in the world. This council notably issued the constitution *Gaudium et spes* on the role of the Church in the modern world.

Secularization: The process of the loss of the influence of religion in individual or social life.

Synod: From the Greek *sunodos* (to travel together), the term for a deliberative ecclesiastical assembly for the purpose of coming to common decisions.

Alexander of Hales (1180–1245)

An English Franciscan philosopher and theologian, known as the *Theologorum monarcha.*

Augustine of Hippo (354–430):

Bishop of Hippo, present-day Annaba, Algeria, a Doctor of the Church and, along with Saints Ambrose of Milan, Jerome, and Gregory the Great, one of the four Western Fathers of the Church.

Ignatius of Loyola (1491–1556):

A Spanish Jesuit, the founder and first superior general of the Society of Jesus, and the author of the *Spiritual Exercises.*

John Paul II (1920–2005):

A Polish pope and prolific author whose works include fourteen encyclicals as well as numerous catecheses about marriage, love, and the family that together are known as the *Theology of the Body.*

King, Martin Luther, Jr. (1929–1968):

An African American Baptist pastor, and non-militant activist for black civil rights in the United States, who was assassinated in Memphis.

Paul of Tarsus (+c. 64–68):

A Pharisee who became an Apostle following the Death and Resurrection of Christ. A tireless missionary to the northern Mediterranean Basin.

Paul VI (1897–1978):

An Italian pope who, on the death of John XXIII, continued the work of the Second Vatican Council.

Paz, Octavio (1914–1998):

A Mexican poet, essayist, diplomat, and winner of the Nobel Prize for Literature.

Pieper, Joseph (1904–1997):

A German Catholic philosopher.

Pius XI (1857–1939):

The 259th pope of the Catholic Church. An Italian, he openly opposed Hitler.

Robert Bellarmine (1542–1621):

An Italian Jesuit and famed theologian.

Sertillanges, Antonin (1863–1948):

A French Dominican moral philosopher.

Thomas Aquinas: (1224–1274):

An Italian Dominican and author of the *Summa Theologiae,* known as the Angelic Doctor.

BOOKS OF THE BIBLE REFERRED TO IN THE APOSTOLIC EXHORTATION

Old Testament

Eccl: The Book of Ecclesiastes

Ex: The Book of Exodus

Jer: The Book of Jeremiah

Mal: The Book of Malachi

Nm: The Book of Numbers

Ps: The Book of Psalms

Song: Song of Songs

Sir: The Book of Sirach

New Testament

Acts: Acts of the Apostles

1 Cor: First Letter to the Corinthians

2 Cor: Second Letter
    to the Corinthians

Eph: Letter to the Ephesians

Gal: Letter to the Galatians

Heb: Letter to the Hebrews

Jas: Letter of James

Jn: The Gospel according to John

Lk: The Gospel according to Luke

Mk: The Gospel according to Mark

Mt: The Gospel according
    to Matthew

Phil: The Letter to the Philippians

1 Pt: The First Letter of Peter

Rom: The Letter to the Romans

1 Thes: The First Letter
    to the Thessalonians

1 Tm: The First Letter of Timothy

Bible references read as follows: Song 11:23; 12:2, 15-18 indicates Song of Songs, chapter 11, verse 23, and chapter 12, verses 2 and 15 to 18.

Publisher: Pierre-Marie Dumont
Vice President, Publishing: Romain Lizé

Pope Francis' text: Chapter 4 of *Amoris Laetitia*
Questions and Reflections: Rev. Arnaud Toury
Translator: Janet Chevrier
Proofreader: Claire Gilligan
Layout and cover: Gauthier Delauné
Iconography: Isabelle Mascaras
Production: Pascale van de Walle, Gwendoline da Rocha
Cover: Pope Francis © Galazka/MP/Leemage.

Printed by Imprimerie Marquis, Canada
Edition number: MGN17016
ISBN: 978-1-941709-41-2

$\mathcal{M}$AGNIFICAT has inspired the prayer lives of millions all over the world....

Why not yours?

$\mathcal{M}$AGNIFICAT *is such a blessing! Once a month I go to the mail box and it's "Christmas." I unwrap each issue and delight in the artwork, the Gospels, and the commentaries written centuries ago as well as those written today. May this joyous, beautiful publication never cease, and may it remain profoundly "Catholic."* Mary L. K.

I just turned 90 in February, but still optimistic, so renewed for another 4 years. Hope God lets me live that long to do his work. Markee B.

I love my MAGNIFICAT. *I'm not even Catholic (yet) but* MAGNIFICAT *is making me want to be. I can't get enough of* MAGNIFICAT. *It is the only thing I do read every day. The print version makes it handy for me and my lifestyle with little kids. Thank you.* Jennifer S.

Ask for a complimentary copy and begin reading and praying with MAGNIFICAT

Receive a FREE COPY *of*
MAGNIFICAT

Please fill out the form below or visit
www.magnificat.com/freecopy

☐ Regular edition
(4.5 x 6.7 inches)

☐ Large print edition
(5 x 7.7 inches)

MY INFORMATION

TITLE   FIRST NAME

LAST NAME

ADDRESS

ADDRESS

CITY

STATE   ZIP   YEAR OF BIRTH

PHONE NUMBER

EMAIL

LOVE17

Offer valid in the US only

Please return this form to
MAGNIFICAT
PO Box 822 – Yonkers, NY 10702

To subscribe for only $44.95 a year,
please visit www.magnificat.com